Copyright © 2015  Publishers

Acknowledgement

The background of the book is very organized. The author of this book has tried to show the use of IPv4 and IPv6 in the current networking protocol scenario. The author has researched and analyzed on the basic and specific features of IPv4 and IPv6 and differentiates these two technology features. The book has been written for the purpose of analyzing the use of IPv6 in the enterprise networking tasks. It has analyzed the advantages and disadvantages of this Enterprise IPv6 technology in an enterprise computer networking. This analysis has researched on enterprise IPv6 network service design, transition mechanisms, and QoS protocol features, etc. In this purposes, the editors of the book have done a great job by providing the necessary information and help to the author. Without their help and effort nothing is possible. The author of this book has been tried to proof all of his work by using the collected research materials. So this book has very in depth background. This book has been written in research based book writing process.

The author doesn't follow traditional technical book writing process. Because he thinks research based technical book writing process is more helpful for article, thesis, book & research paper etc. writing. And this process makes a book easy to understand to its reader.

So by reading the book a reader can easily understand the topics of the book and he/she can easily gather the ideas about how to write general, non-general thesis paper, research paper, report, article and technical assignment, etc. The author hopes his book will be helpful for the future research on Enterprise IPv6 for enterprise networking purposes.

Abstract

The traditional enterprise network for IPv6 transition mechanisms has been IPv4 address reduction, which is speeding up due to the development of Internet connection particularly in Asia & EU. Prior to 2007, IPv6 address allowance guidelines were totally observed and permitted only for the enterprises to acquire a network address from a single service agency to prevent overlapping of the international routing methods. This has modified since 2007, where enterprises can now get Provider Independence (PI) allocations just like that of IPv4. When an enterprise is applicable for PI field, it can acquire IPv6 address space that is not connected with any organization.

However, many new components are in the developing stage and plan are being mentioned in the market that can affect how multiple networking is done with IPv6. Nowadays there are some unanswered concerns relevant to this subject, and people should observe the factors of a network and get in touch with their companies, as time goes on to stay upgraded with these changes.

Enterprise IPv6 for Enterprise Networks

Authored by: Ghazi Mokammel Hossain

Editing and Proofread by: i. Mohammed Fathe Mubin ii. Mike Westley iii. Jason Donald

Preface by: Rayne Alfred Collins

Designed by: Ghazi Mokammel Hossain

Publications Format: Amazon Kindle E-Book format, Amazon Createspace Paper back format

Edition No: Second Edition, December, 2015

Publication From: USA

Version: International Version

Published by: GM Publishers, associated with Amazon Kindle Direct Publishing & Createspace

ISBN-13: 978-1519223784

ISBN-10: 1519223781 (The book has been assigned a CreateSpace ISBN)

Email address: gmpublishers04@gmail.com

GM Publishers

My Book My Life

Table of Contents

1.0 Introduction

Internet Protocol version 6 (IPv6) is the next edition of the Cisco Internet Protocol (IP), that is used for connecting all kinds of devices on the internet. IPv6 has been existing for many decades, but the implementation of IPv6 has introduced significantly on the enterprise in the recent time period. IPv6 has been reveled in developing stage and it is developing as real-world deployments reveal in either the protocol or the implementation strategy of the protocol.

Enterprises all over the world are connected to IPv6 by both implementing and operating the network as well as applications that instantly use IPv6 (sometimes using it without knowing it properly) or they are proactively implementing IPv6. Though the existence of IPv6 was found for a number of years, the implementation of IPv6 has created a new era in the enterprise world. Most of the companies all over the world are taking necessary action to implement their operating system and applications to analyze IPv6. These applications mostly use IPv6, sometimes using it without knowing it properly.

For getting extra working bandwidth, more growth at the marketplace, experiencing with merger-&-acquisition difficulties and to utilize different abilities of the protocol to cut-edge application and endpoints, most of the enterprises are trying to implement IPv6 with complete features (Solomon and Kunath, 2011).

Whatever the purpose, it is hard for any enterprise to completely comprehend the implementation choices available for IPv6 and to take a competitive but well-thought-out preparation and design strategy for their implementation (Bagnulo and Baker, 2008). With a vision to connect all the devices of the internet, Internet Protocol version 6 (IPv6) is thought as the subsequent version of the protocol being used.

A number of researchers have recommended implementing the different options of IPv6 at the shortest possible time without analyzing the purpose of implementation. It is also suggested to choose a competitive and strategic network design for the enterprise before implementation (Bagnulo and Baker, 2008). Sufficient time is required to analyze the capability of all the existing methodologies of IPv6. It is impossible to upgrade IPv4 similar to IPv6 in a shortest possible time. A number of errors are observed in IPv6 while analyzing from IPv4. Organizational system also obstruct the implementation of such a new system in considering several risk factors involved in it. An absence of IPv6 is also observed in this case. It is also a big challenge to convert all the programs, devices so that they can understand IPv6. The greatest risks of mismatching the application with the devices exist in this case (Cisco.com, 2014).

All these factors have encouraged the researches to find an alternate solution for supporting the IPv4, which exists at present and developing IPv6 in such a way so that it completely adjusts with the requirement of the enterprise.

The main objective of this analysis is to provide a broad scenario for the technological development related to implementation of IPv6 in an ideal way in the networking system of the organization. There exist a number of options for further research. A number of factors are involved with the implementation of the system. Further technical development and innovation is required to make a connection between IPv4 and IPv6 to ensure a complete solution for an enterprise (Hinden and Deering, 2003). The effectiveness and efficiency level of the innovative technologies can also be measured by conducting further research to align it with the exact requirement of the enterprise.

Implementation of IPv6 according to the necessity of the enterprise is the main concern of this research (IPv6 security issues). The analysis will also include the research findings of the IPv6 technology for the networking system in a different organization.

The need of sufficient time is to allow IPv6 capabilities on all present networking technologies. However, IPv4 network cannot upgrade to IPv6 network rapidly. This is partially due to the specific limitations of IPv6 as in conversion to IPv4. Also, organizations are incredibly risk-averse and are not tuned into new changes so rapidly. Furthermore, there is a lack of interest in IPv6 up gradation. The specific incompatibilities to convert all the devices to synchronize IPv6 rapidly. It is another issue that must be met. These factors force us to look for the alternatives that support co-existence methods of IPv4 and IPv6 in the enterprise network scenario (Cisco.com, 2014).

This analysis provides an extensive advantages of IPv6 technology ideal for an enterprise network system. There are several ideas for further research. The ideas that were not described are placed in need of further research. In particular, further research on technology that allows IPv4 servers to connect with IPv6 servers and applications are required (Hinden and Deering, 2003). Furthermore, each of the recommended technology could also be further examined by analyzing the efficiency and implementation issues.

So this analysis concentrates on the implementation of enterprise IPv6 technology. It also reveals and presents the research outcome on the IPv6 technology for enterprise networking.

1.1 General Question

As the entire world doesn't know too much about 'IPv6' or 'Enterprise IPv6' so there are lots of queries arise about this new technology. The entrepreneurs as well as the enterprise or business organization related persons are always trying to know about the answers of these queries.

The most common query about IPv6 is given below: Nowadays the enterprise professionals ask a common question about the Enterprise IPv6 the question is as follows:

What are the challenges in rolling out IPv6 across an enterprise network?

The author of this book has tried hard to find out the answer of this common question in the following parts of this book.

1.2 Aims of the Analysis

1. To find out the enterprise IPv6 technology in an enterprise computer networking environment

2. To analyze the advantages and disadvantages of this Enterprise IPv6 technology in an enterprise computer networking system

3. To provide the result, recommendations and summary of the research analysis

4. To differentiate between IPv4 and IPv6

5. To research the structure of the enterprise IPv6 technology

6. To research the features of enterprise IPv6

7. To analyze the existing IPv6 technology in the networking system of different enterprises

8. To understand the structure and main features of IPv6 existing in different enterprises

9. To distinguish between the loss and advantage faced by an enterprise in establishing IPv6 technology in their computer networking system

10. To lash out some sorts of result from the analysis and summarizing the findings

11. To know some recommendations for the system development

1.3 Objectives of the Analysis

- To provide the best recommendation about the enterprise IPv6 technology for enterprise networking solutions
- To find out the advantages and disadvantages IPv6 technology as compared to IPv4 technology for enterprise networking
- To fully under-stand about this technology

1.4 Research Flow Diagram

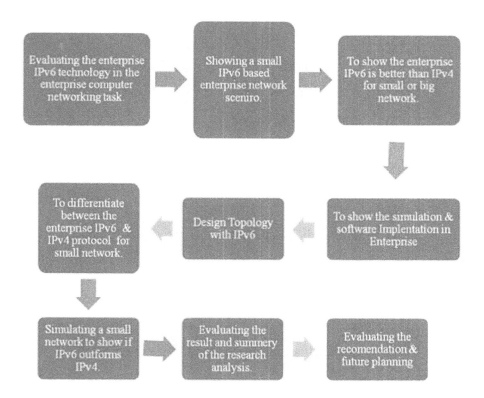

1.5 Structure of the Analysis

✓ **Introduction:** The Introduction of the analysis is composed of the basic and compact knowledge given on IPv4, IPv6 along with various information about enterprise IPv6.

✓ **Literature Review:** It shares some previous ideas, researches done by some other authors. Even some personal opinion and examples were also added in this part. It discusses how relevant the topic of the research is provided with which we are working with.

✓ **The main body of the Analysis**: This part of the research explains and discusses about the artefact in addresses. It forms the logical and analytical background of the research. This part mainly evaluates how the research is relevant and how the aims and objectives can be reached through the use of enterprise IPv6. Finally, some recommendations are also provided in this part along with the summary of the result obtained during the research.

✓ **Conclusion:** It discusses about the end of the research.

✓ **Critical Evaluation:** It surveys the every aspect very carefully and observes it every procedure step by step. It also compares how much fruitful will the research be and finally also includes self-evaluation after doing the research.

✓ **Reference and Bibliography**

2.0 Literature Review

IPv6 is the next generation protocol of the Internet that take over the address restrictions of IPv4 and eliminates or decreases the situations for NAT/PAT as they are used nowadays. The key factors of IPv6 is the variety of IP addresses. This escalates the growth of the enterprise and create the way for new applications across the Internet.

The Internet Engineering Task Force (IETF) and other companies keep finding alternatives and produce rights and RFCs to make sure the interoperability of IPv6-enabled servers (Sholomon and Kunath, 2011). Almost all companies and device suppliers, and many enterprises, are preparing, implementing, or have implemented IPv6 within their networks for developing the future network structures and applications (Lawson, 2011).

While many enterprises are ready to allow IPv6 or setup plans for the implementation of IPv6, some of the enterprise such as Retail store, Production companies, Web 2.0 and Enterprise, IT companies are playing major roles to adopt both by allowing network and computers to support IPv6 and also allowing their enterprise applications for IPv6 (Draves, 2003). The internet has developed from an internal allocated processing application used by the U.S. Department of Defense as a method that allows an enterprise or organization to be efficient and more effective in offering products or services to its international clients (Draves, 2003).

Enterprise applications have progressed over the decades from the easiest method of client/server to make it more user friendly. Nowadays, these enterprise applications can use technology such as speech, video and wireless internet network (Bagnulo and Baker, 2008). The adaptation of collaborative, entertaining applications has made a significant move in the understanding and the needs of the enterprise network.

The changing enterprise scenario now requires the enterprise network to provide the following:

- **Customer experience for enterprise related applications:** The use of enterprise real-time connection, single-sign-in, and flexibility apps is in implementing stage, with a positive and attractive consumer orientation being one of the main concerns.

- **Supporting different types of device & gadgets:** Enterprises are experiencing an increase adaptation of Wi-Fi devices (including Wi-Fi-enabled notebooks, tabs and smart phones) and the client devices in addition to the traditional PC and IP phones.

- **Network resiliency and time management:** Enterprise operations that related to globalization and continue to operate 24/7 hours, all year round. It requires a long lasting network system that guarantees accessibility enterprise applications during a network update or failing (Rooney, 2011).

- **High security:** Over the decades, security risks have developed in a large number and complex form, requiring the network security to develop and support allocated and powerful application environments.

The need of versatile client and traffics accessibility is increasing as the development of the new types of enterprise. The enterprise network is a system that interconnects end users and devices. It can connect only one place or several places in a developing, or several structures across a geographical area. The enterprise network is a high-speed system that provides basic connection and offers a long lasting, secure, easy-to-manage network services which needed to run enterprise-critical applications. IPv6 based Enterprise network is developed to maintain three principles (Rooney, 2011):

- Modularity
- Structure
- Resiliency

- **Modularity:** Modularity is one of the essential concepts of an organize network that describes the enterprise network as a setup of several foundations, developed independently using a methodical strategy and implementing structure and redundancy where appropriate. Improved modularity in a network design has a self-contained network recover to back up a particular or set of features.

Therefore, a failure, update, upgrade or any modify in one component will be restricted to its own limitations. With a flip network design, network services can be chosen on a per-module structure, but would need to be verified as part of the overall network design.

- **Structure:** Structure is one of the key medium of support for a good network design. Each component described in the previous area needs, having hierarchy and resiliency designed into the network model. For the enterprise environment and actual connection to proceed to evolve, the network design must be flexible enough to support brand new devices, apps and programs, or improve potential without going through a significant fork lift update.

This network design versatility has been progressed from the traditional network to a hierarchical topology with distinct levels, where each part has a particular part that allows the network architect to choose the right network and allows the needed features for that part.

These levels have efficient features and provide limitations to failure domains. Each part has exclusive features and individual segments for managing network services.

- **Resiliency:** Moreover to design a perfect enterprise network structure, it is important for network architects to consider resiliency in every step of the network design. Developing resiliency to prevent every criteria of failing is a key factor in guaranteeing high accessibility and enterprise growth. The synchronize uses of resiliency can be sustained within the change. Web connect, and network designs are required across all the different segments and levels that have been mentioned previously.

For example, allowing repetitive application in the accessibility part can ensure the enterprise growth even if the effective application is not able to find out the definite result. This ensures that there is no effect in network connection on the submission port (for both Layer 2 and routed accessibility deployments). Including resiliency to the design might require the use of new features, but it is often just an issue of how you choose to apply your structure and how you setup the primary Layer 2 and Layer 3 topologies.

The following table shows the difference between IPv4 and IPv6 in an enterprise scenario which has mainly focused on the necessity in rolling out IPv6 across enterprise networks:

Comparison	
IPv4	IPv6
Source and destination addresses are 32 bits (4 bytes) in length.	Source and destination addresses are 128 bits (16 bytes) in length.
IPsec support is optional.	IPSec is mandatory and end-to-end.
Identification of packet flow for QoS handling by routers is absent within the IPv4 header.	Packet flow identification for QoS handling by routers is included in the IPv6 header using the flow label field.
Fragmentation is performed by both routers and the sending host.	Fragmentation is not done by routers, only the sending host.
Header includes a checksum.	Header does not include a checksum.
Header includes options.	All optional data is moved to IPv6 extension headers.
Address Resolution Protocol (ARP) uses broadcast ARP request frames to resolve an IPv4 address to a link layer address.	ARP Request frames are replaced with multicast neighbor solicitation messages.
Internet Group Management Protocol (IGMP) is used to manage local subnet group membership.	IGMP is replaced with Multicast Listener Discovery (MLD) messages.
ICMP Router Discovery is used to determine the IPv4 address of the best default gateway and is optional.	ICMP Router Discovery is replaced with ICMPv6 Router Solicitation and Router Advertisement messages and is required.
Broadcast addresses are used to send traffic to all nodes on a subnet.	There are no IPv6 broadcast addresses. Instead, a linklocal scope all-nodes multicast address is used.
Must be configured either manually or through DHCP.	Does not require manual configuration or DHCP.
Uses host address (A) resource records in the Domain Name System (DNS) to map host names to IPv4 addresses.	Uses host address (AAA) resource records in the Domain Name System (DNS) to map host names to IPv6 addresses.
Uses pointer (PTR) resource records in the INADDR.ARPA DNS domain to map IPv4 addresses to host names.	Uses pointer (PTR) resource records in the IP6.ARPA DNS domain to map IPv6 addresses to host names.
Must support a 576-byte packet size (possibly fragmented).	Must support a 1280-byte packet size (without fragmentation).

Figure 1: Difference between IPv4 and IPv6 in enterprise scenario

Enterprise related works often get slowdown due to the organizational problems and validation for a new venture. And often end up with a technological design and execution that is procured to figure it out "as we go along" mind-set. The objective of this book is to give people a realistic and confirmed way to figure out the larger process of IPv6 implementation into usable segments based on locations in the network and to provide users with verified settings examples that can be used to develop enterprise, and manufacture network design (Hossain, 2013).

Industry research that often happens on the outside of the enterprise area as time pressured upon an enterprise from the marketplace, they are in or by other external causes (for example, Internet IPv4 address exhaustion), whereas others are valuable to the enterprise depending on enterprise or technological advantages (Hossain, 2013).

There are three key factors why companies might need IPv6 (Lawson, 2011):

- Need for a larger address space (beyond IPv4) for an enterprise to help the organization in its continual and increasing development. IPv6 is also a pioneer of new possibilities and a system of advancement.

- There are some of network applications that are not operate with IPv4 for example, vehicle-mounted GPS system, which might include a large number of network receivers on cars.

- IPv6 is best match for the operating-system like Microsoft Windows 7, 8, 8.1, 10, Pro, Enterprise Edition and Linux based operating network system.

Developed nations like India and China have large communities and increasing technological proficiency, will almost certainly shift to IPv6. Enterprises that want to be effective in those marketplaces but do not use IPv6 will be faced rapid drawback. Internet Protocol version 6 (IPv6) is the latest adjustment of the Internet Protocol (IP), the protocol that provides an identification and program for computer and puts users across the Internet. IPv6 was designed by the Internet Engineering Task Force (IETF) to solve the long-anticipated problem of IPv4 address exhaustion (Cisco.com, 2014).

However, the only Quality of Service (QoS) network designed into IPv6 has a few headers areas that are expected to be used to differentiate packets that belong to various sessions of traffics and to recognize related packets as a "flow." The objective is that these headers areas should allow devices such as routers to recognize moves and types of traffics and do fast transfer of data on them. The use of these header components is optionally available, which means that many devices do not hassle with anything other than the lowest amount of support required. However, IPv4 has identical header components, designed to be used in identical ways, so it can be declared that IPv6 QoS is better than IPv4 (Cisco.com, 2014).

It would be more precise to say that IPv6 is not less or not more secured than IPv4 it is just totally different. The primary security-related procedure integrated into the IPv6 structure is IPsec. Any RFC-based, standards-compliant execution of IPv6 must use IPsec, however, there is no need that the performance is allowed or used. This has led to the false impression that IPv6 is more secured than IPv4. Instead, it still needs careful execution and a well-establish application and programmers. This is mostly a belief because of Network Address Transition (NAT) improves security level. NAT prevails to take over a lack of IPv4 addresses, and because IPv6 has no lack, IPv6 networks do not need NAT. To those who see NAT as security, this seems to mean a lack in the security of IPv6. However, NAT does not provide any significant security.

The mind-set of security through obscurity is mostly an obsolete idea because many strikes or hack do not occur through straight routable IP based system from the internet into the inside of the enterprise but rather through Levels 4–7 strikes.

IPv6 was developed with the objective of making NAT needless, and RFC 4864 describes the idea of Native Network Protection (LNP) using IPv6 this provides the same or better security advantages than NAT (McFarland, 2011). IPv6 is designed for alternative IPv4, which still provides many internet traffics as of 2013. As of September 2013, the amount of clients getting Google services over IPv6 surpassed 2% for the first time.

Every program on the internet must be assigned an IP address in order to connect to other devices (McFarland, 2011). With the ever-increasing number of new devices being connected to the Internet, the need happened with more data than IPv4 is able to offer.

Why and when an enterprise should consider IPv6:

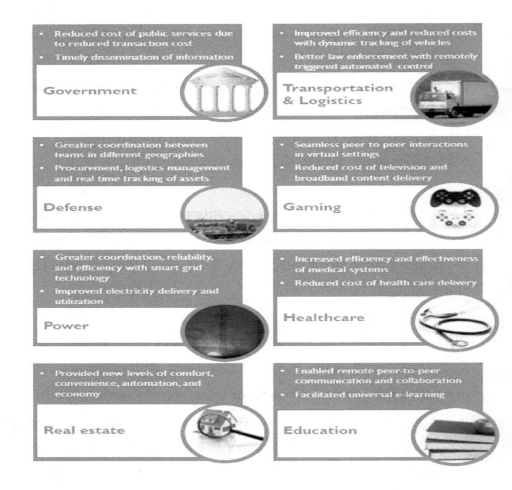

Figure 2: IPv6 advantages for various industry sectors

The Development of Internet World and The Need of IPv6: Last few years IPv4 were nicely implemented on various types of networking system like, enterprise or organizational networking purposes. So right now, Cisco is trying to implement their new Internet Protocol on various enterprises and organizational fields.

This area concentrates on the current alternatives that increase the life of the internet and the advantages that IPv6 provides over other alternatives (Cisco.com, 2014). The following chart of IPv6 growth statistics can clear the growing popularity and need of IPv6:

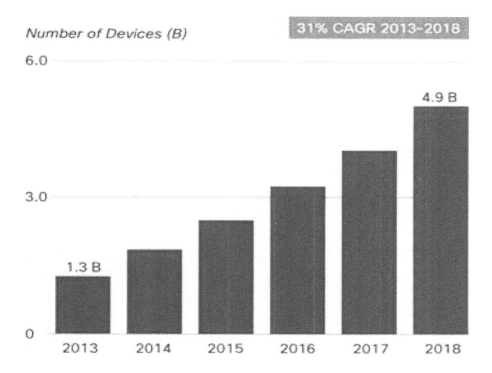

Figure: IPv6 growth statistics in recent and upcoming years

IPv6 in the IETF: As IPv6 goes popular, it is important for the standards bodies to clarify about the technology to its users. For example, Internet Engineering Task Force (IETF) to standardize on these abilities, which can be implemented across all networks and the computers.

Enterprise IPv6 Implementation Status: While many enterprises are preparing to allow IPv6 or setup plans for the implementation of IPv6, some of the enterprise such as Retail store, Production, Web 2.0 and Enterprise IT companies are major to adopting both by allowing programs and computers to support IPv6 and also allowing their organizational network over IPv6 (McFarland, 2011).

You have already known that, the Internet has evolved from an internal distributed computing network used by the U.S. Department of Defense with a medium that enables enterprises to be innovative and more productive in providing goods and services to its global customers (McFarland, 2011). The Internet Protocol Suite (TCP/IP) is the actual technology used to allow this network connection.

Although the online network doesn't maintain any legal governance it does have overreaching organizations that help to apply and sustain policy and function of key internet components such as the IP address space and Domain Name System (DNS). These components are controlled and regulated by the Internet Corporation for Assigned Names and Numbers (ICANN), which operates the Internet Assigned Numbers Authority (IANA) (McFarland, 2011).

ICANN/IANA assigns unique identifiers for use on the Internet, (IANA) which include domains, Internet Protocol (IP), and Application Port Numbers (APN) (Kim, 2011).

Typical Customer Roadmap for IPv6 transition

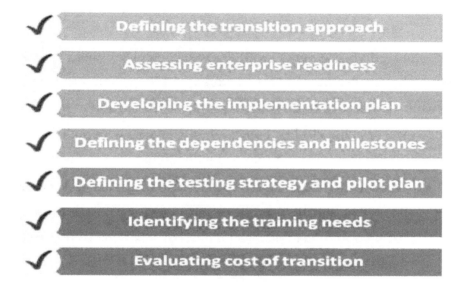

Figure 3: Steps prior to IPv6 transition implementation

The present IPv4-based address design will not be enough to provide the increasing address needs of the enterprise network process. IPv6 has been developed to address this deficiency. However, the task is how to add IPv6 to an enterprise network successfully and with the least effect. Various networks have been suggested to accomplish this.

Native IPv6 (IPv6-only networks) represents the network where IPv6 is the only medium of protocol that's operating. IPv6 and Enterprise have Coexistence Mechanisms which have some extraordinary transition mechanism features. As the name indicates, transition mechanisms help in the conversion from one protocol to another. In the viewpoint of IPv6, transition mechanism generally indicates shifting from IPv4 to IPv6 (Bouras, Karaliotas and Ganos, 2003).

In future, IPv6 networks will absolutely replace today's IPv4 protocol. For the near future, a variety of transition mechanism networks are needed to allow both protocols to function at the same time (McFarland, 2011). Some of the most commonly used transition mechanisms are mentioned in the following segments:

- **Dual-stack:** Dual-stack represents the host/network where both IPv4 and IPv6 protocols are operating on the devices. As IPv4 also has this technology, but this is more backward than IPv6 Dual-stack technology.

- **IPv6 over IPv4 tunnels:** This transition mechanism provides IPv6 packets are exemplified within an IPv4 packet. This strategy is used where IPv6 networks are separated and IPv4 is the only choice to transverse over the present network. In this situation, IPv6 is preferable and have more advantages than IPv4 (Kim, 2011).

- **IPv6 over MPLS:** In this transition mechanism, the IPv6 websites connect with professional IPv6 websites over an IPv4 Multiprotocol Label Switching (MPLS) offering more powerful and greater efficiency.

- **Transition mechanisms:** By using the transition mechanisms like Socks gateway, Network Address Transition-Port Transition (NAT-PT), TCP-UDP Relay, and NAT64 the IPv6-only devices, devices can communicate with the IPv4-only devices or gadgets (Kim, 2011).

Another new feature of IPv6 is Stateless Address Auto Configuration (SLAAC), "built in" IPsec, mobile IPv6, flow label, and more. The lead provides the best probability to assess these functions. Each enterprise can use some or all of these new features. An in-depth knowing of these functions will help on identifying IPv6 guidelines for enterprises. As an example, SLAAC allows hosts to acquire an IPv6 address instantly when connected to a routed IPv6 network. However, this might be inappropriate for an application, where a stateful settings using DHCPv6 or the fixed IPv6 address might have to be used (Bouras, Karaliotas and Ganos, 2003). Enterprise IPv6 protocol has Quality of Service (QoS) protocol features which is another important protocol features of enterprise IPv6. Because enterprise networks of today's world are designed to be complicated international networking infrastructures (Sholomon and Kunath, 2011).

These networks have the system to enable lots of applications, programs and services. QoS protocol has the process of offering different application sources with nodes and analytics such as (Kim, 2011):

- Bandwidth
- Delay
- Interpacket wait difference (jitter)
- Packet loss

However, the enterprises are facing the above challenges at the time of rolling out IPv6 on their network infrastructure. There are many limitations of IPv4 in compare with IPv6, The following figure has shown the limitations of IPv4 in enterprise or organizational uses:

Figure 4: IPv4 Limitations

The Benchmark of IPv4 against IPv6:

This part has shown the benchmark of IPv4 against IPv6 in a small table they are as follows:

Features	Benchmark of IPv4	Benchmark of IPv6
1.Addresses	IPv4 address is only 32 bit long.	IPv6 address is 128 bits long which has much bigger memory size than IPv4.
2.Address setting	Stateful-address settings are just like the current DHCP performance in IPv4.	IPv6 provides both a stateful and stateless address settings operationality. It also supports Stateless Address Auto Configuration (SLAAC).
3.ICMP	Besides the primary ICMP information found in IPv4. ARP performance in IPv4 has successfully been changed with The Internet Control Message Protocol (ICMP Kinds 135 & 136) and Wireless router Finding (ICMP Kinds 133 & 134) messages. To sustain in reverse interface with IPv4, the expansion headers comprehend many conventional IP method figures (such as IPv6 for TCP).	ICMP is an essential element of IPv6. It features several new ICMP information. IPv6 features several new ICMP messages.

4.Packet Structure	These conventional IPv4 method headers must occur as the last expansion headers in the connected record since they do not have a Next Header area in those.	The basic IPv6 headline has been structured to only contain the following fields: Edition, Traffic, Class, Circulation Brand, Payload Length, Next Header, Hop Restrict, Source address and Location address. Routers can process this structured headers more effectively.
5.Speed Benchmark	In 1GB/s Ethernet connection IPv4 can reach 100MB/s because of its small memory size, the protocol processing speed is very fast than IPv6.	In 1GB/s Ethernet connection IPv6 can rich 84MB/s because of its huge memory size, the protocol processing speed is much slower than IPv4.

So this analysis shows the enterprises and organizations with a design structure to assist them in shifting to IPv6 through a transition mechanism and explains the ways of developing IPv6 into their current network infrastructures.

The analysis also concentrates on the implementation of enterprise IPv6 technology. It also reveals the detail research outcomes of the IPv6 technology for enterprise networking.

3.0 Detail Discussion of the Artifact

The detailed analyses of the artifact are as follows:

- IPv6 follows some definite network design structure. Enterprise campus network design is one of them, which has two basic layers, i. Distribution layer and ii. Access layer. With the help of these two layers the network model works. Enterprise network services design is relatively new design which also provides some more new features than the previous design.

- Enterprise core network is probably the easiest as well as the hardest design at the same time. The core layer helps in layer 3 routing for the traffic's in and out. Instead, Enterprise data center network is almost similar to the campus network with some minor differences. It depends on two layers i. Aggregate layer and ii. Access layer. Enterprise edge network design is rather more dependent on the internet, VPN and WAN based networks. Typical branch network design is on the other hand more suitable function of branches.

- A common IPv6 co-existences mechanism discusses all the mechanisms in the network designs. It discusses all about how the user can switch or convert the protocol to a different protocol. For example, Dual-Stack is one of the best recommended protocol transitions. The tunneling is used as a tunneler between IPv6 and IPv4 in WAN.

- The tunneling network uses some function for backup the Novell IPX/SPX, AppleTalk, SNA, and others.

- Protocol transition mechanism includes some examples like NAT-PT, NAT64 etc.

- Different types of network services are also discussed briefly.

- Deployment of IPv6 network includes different types of deployment ideas. Of these ideas, Campus Networks was chosen for practical research use by the imaginary 'ABC Enterprise'. And Dual Stack Model (DSM) was chosen as the model for the deployment of the network design.

- Finally, some recommendations has been discussed which the Enterprise should be aware of.

Design

3.1 Enterprise IPv6 Network Design

As Enterprise IPv6 is the modern version of the IPv4 so lots of new network models are added in this upgraded version. The Enterprise IPv6 follows some network model design infrastructures which are discussed below:

3.1.1 Enterprise Campus Network Design

The architecture of this design has a basic block that connected it through the core of the network:

- Distribution Layer
- Access Layer

- **Distribution Layer:** Distribution layer interconnects the access layer part switch to the core of the networking process (McFarland, 2011). A large enterprise campus network may have one or more distribution switch, based on the number of downstream access layer part switch connected with it. The best methods recommend, not going beyond 20 access layer switch connected with a single distribution part. This is mostly limited by the control planning and controlling module of the distribution layer part, whether it is a Layer 2 or direct routed access design (Bouras, Karaliotas and Ganos, 2003).

There are three types of Distribution Layer:

➢ Layer 2 access design

➢ Routed access design

➢ Virtual switch design

- **Access Layer:** Access layer is the primary feature of contact or edge of the enterprise network. This part is the feature where, devices connect to access the networking process. The access part also shows as the primary place where network services can be started. PC, web servers, IP cell phones, wireless access points, IP cameras, and other PoE/PoE+ devices are examples of a wide variety of devices that can get connected to the access layer network (Kim, 2011).

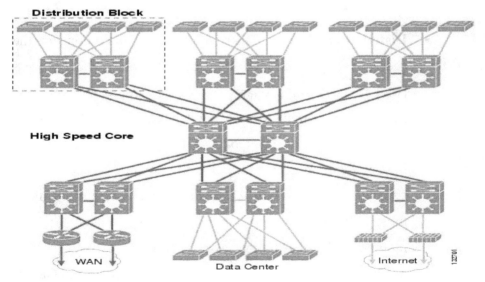

Figure 5: Enterprise Campus Network Design of Enterprise IPv6

3.1.2 Enterprise Network Services Design

The network service component is relatively a new feature of the campus design. As enterprise campus network organizers start to consider shift to dual-stack IPv4/IPv6 environments, and keep incorporate to more innovative Unified Communications services, a number of difficulties can be found due to this shifting process (Sholomon and Kunath, 2011). It will be essential to bring these solutions into the campus network effectively, while analyzing the appropriate level of operational changes in management and error solving. Enterprise Network Services Design provides following facilities to its users:

- Central Wireless Controllers: These features remotely operate and organize access points across the entire campus.

- Centralized IPv6 Intra-Site Automatic Tunnel Addressing Protocol (ISATAP) tunnel cancellations from the enterprise campus to the network solutions module: This develops a firmly managed overlay tunnel network on top of the existing network process. Like all the tunneling technology, running multiple ISATAP channels to different sections in the network increases network administration flexibility along with making it extremely hard to manage and repair the network system (Kim, 2011).

- Unified Communications services (Cisco Unified Communications Manager, gateways): Unified

Communications services enable the enterprise setup communication managers and other Speech-generating devices (SGDs) devices and applications in the service block for centralized gateway.

- Plan gateways: Plan gateways provide user verification and authorization along with Network Access Control (NAC) functions. Plan gateways include authentication, permission, and data analytics web servers, accessibility management servers and it also manages NAC profilers.

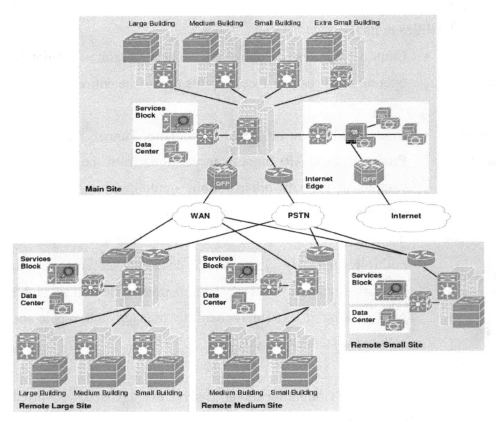

Figure 6: Enterprise Network Services Design of Enterprise IPv6

3.1.3 Enterprise Core Network Design

Core layer is the normal, but the most crucial part of a network design. This part is the central source of the network. The core layer needs to be more efficient and switch high traffic as quick as possible. It provides a restricted set of services and uses repetitive devices and features to make sure that the software updates or components switch can be made without interfering with the applications. Core layer provides a Layer 3 routing component for all the traffics in and out of the enterprise network. Routing is difficult to the data centre core and would need to be designed using built-in effective security procedure to avoid wrong next door neighbour peering injection of wrong channels, and routing loops (McFarland, 2011).

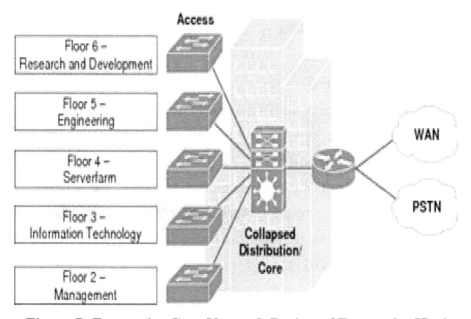

Figure 7: Enterprise Core Network Design of Enterprise IPv6

3.1.4 Enterprise Data Center Network Design

The Data center design almost similar to an enterprise campus network design with a few exclusions, such as a few functions and features and efficiency variations. But the routing and switching process are almost same. It has following layers:

- **Aggregation layer:** This layer is the cancellation point for the access layer and joins the data center network to the enterprise core network. In other designs, enterprises consider core to be also part of the data center, but the design principles still stay the same for the core layer part. In the data center design, the aggregation layer works as a service layer that provides Layer 4 to Layer 7 services such as security (firewall), Server Load Balancing (SLB), and channeling solutions.

- **Access layer:** This layer can be a physical access layer part using the Driver and Nexus switches, or it can be virtually a control layer by using the hypervisor-based software switch such as the 'cisco Nexus 1000v'. Access layer can join any virtual devices and bare-metal web servers to the network. It generally joins to the servers using 10/100/1000 connections with uplink to the distribution at 10 Gbps rates of speed (McFarland, 2011).

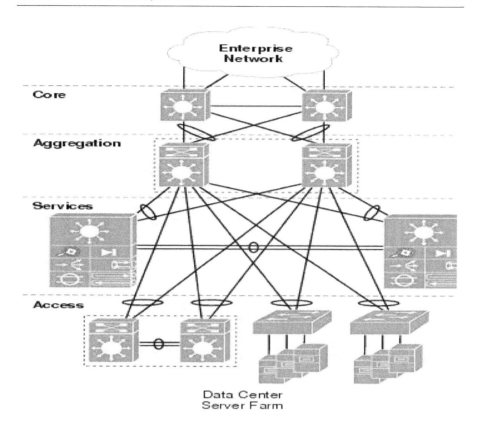

Figure 8: Enterprise Data Center Network Design of Enterprise IPv6

3.1.5 Enterprise Edge Network Design

Enterprise edge network includes the Internet, Virtual Private Network (VPN), and WAN (Wide Area Network) that connect an enterprise to a service agency network. Enterprise edge module provides all the network elements for efficient and secure connections between the enterprise campus, data center, and distant places, associates, mobile users, and the online users (Amoss and

Minoli,2008). The edge network for an enterprise has three following key network features:

- The enterprise head office, which is commonly known as the WAN aggregation network center.
- The division side to get connected to the WAN aggregation network.
- The area that experiencing the Internet, which provides both distant VPN and regular Internet access.

The enterprise edge network aggregates the connection from the various distant sites, filtration of traffics, and route the traffic into the enterprise. The topological design of edge network enables versatility and personalization to meet the needs of different types of customers and their specific enterprise models.

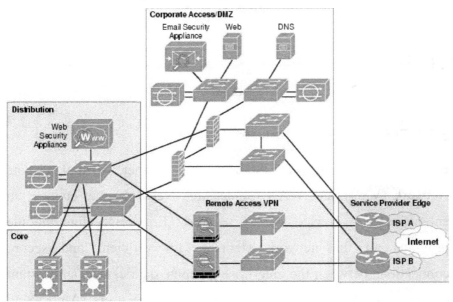

Figure 9: Enterprise Edge Network Design of Enterprise IPv6

3.1.6 Typical Branch Network Design

Based on the size of the branch, each branch network would require an external connectivity up to 1.5 Megabyte per second for small branches (up to 100 users) or high-speed (up to 45 Mbps) for larger branches. In other designs, enterprise can use conventional private WAN network such as MPLS or Frame Relay, or they can leverage the Internet. They can use the Internet by connecting distant sites using VPN (Kim, 2011). Typical Branch Network Design has layer 2 access switch which has the following key features:

✓ Power over Ethernet (PoE).
✓ Spanning Tree.
✓ Class of Service (CoS) on access ports and QoS policing and shaping on edge routers.

The branch router hosts the following facilities:

- **Security services:** Security services such as firewalls and IPsec are either incorporated or applied to an individual device based on the amount of traffic that execute at the branch.

- Integrated modules inside of the edge router can offer service, or a standalone device such as a 'CISO' ASA Firewall application can be used (Bouras, Karaliotas and Ganos, 2003).

- **Unified Communications services:** These services include native call control, FXO/FXS slots for direct Public Switched Telephone Network (PSTN) connection (emergency 911), and back-up connectivity.

- **Program intellect services:** One of the goals of the branch service network is to offer branch network user with the same network features and support levels as an enterprise user.

- This can be difficult because of the restricted data transfer bandwidth and natural delay in WAN hyper connects.

- A typical small branch which has restricted WAN data transfer bandwidth can significantly advantage from application intellect service, such as WAN optimization/application speed up using the 'CISO' WAAS (McFarland, 2011).

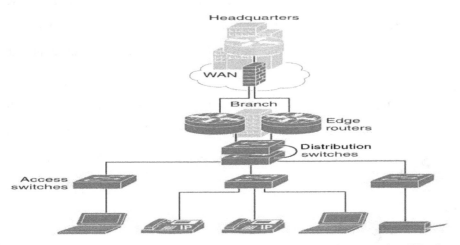

Figure 10: Typical Branch Network Design of Enterprise IPv6

Implementation

3.2 Enterprise IPv6 Coexistence

Mechanisms

In the above part of this book, the author has shown Enterprise IPv6 various network design structures. Now the author will present the implementation of enterprise IPv6 in an imaginary enterprise network environment. In this part he will also discuss on Common IPv6 Coexistence Mechanisms. Common IPv6 Coexistence Mechanisms are a cluster of Native IPv6, Transition mechanisms, Dual-Stack, IPv6 over IPv4 tunnels, and IPv6 over MPLS and Transition mechanisms. There are various types of Common IPv6 Coexistence Mechanisms their discussions are as follows:

3.2.1 Native IPv6

The Native IPv6 is also known as "IPv6-only." It is essentially implying that IPv6 is the only operating IP protocol in the network. In normal conditions, the IPv6 environments can be thought of in the same way as native IPv4 environments of the present days, only using a high level of IP. There will be a time when the operating and investment cost for operating a dual-stack network will become unjustifiable (Kim, 2011). In some cases and that case will vary from network to network, it may be a best decision to completely turn off IPv4 or at least in most of the networks.

There are already some clients who setup a native IPv6 network on their new enterprise where the network and application technologies are also assisting IPv6 with few to no holes in operational advantage (Amoss and Minoli, 2008).

The size of these networks are tiny, but they will rise eventually. IPv6 allows enterprises or companies to setup applications address in particular enterprise needs. However, the biggest task is the implementation of native IPv6 in the near future. It is true that, not everyone is participating in this implementation process. Additional difficulties consist of the lack of end-to-end and effective IPv6 assistance in the network, security, control, management, and applications. Most of the large organizations or enterprises have designed exclusive applications, to analyzing the operational difficulties for the conversion to IPv6 (Kim, 2011). This scenario is appropriate for the enterprises. Native IPv6 deployments will nicely flourish as the supporting problems or gaps are filled by the providers and enterprises.

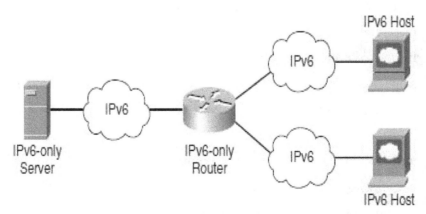

Figure 11: Native IPv6 topology

3.2.2 Transition Mechanisms

Transition mechanisms help in the conversion from one protocol to another. In the viewpoint of IPv6, transition generally indicates shifting from IPv4 to IPv6. In future IPv6 networks will absolutely substitute today's IPv4 technology (Amoss and Minoli, 2008). For the near future, a variety of transition mechanisms are needed to allow both protocols to operate at the same time.

Dual-stack

Dual-stack is the basic and recommended IPv4-to-IPv6 transition mechanism. Dual-stack provides the most accurate way for IPv6 servers and networks to be implemented because no tunneling or interpretation needs to be conducted for end-to-end connection. In a dual-stack implementation, both IPv4 and IPv6 are operational on all elements (hosts, servers, routers, switches, firewalls, and so on) connected to the network. The dual-stack procedure has been also used in past times.

Previous examples of this mechanism includes IPv4 with IPX and/or AppleTalk coexisting on the same node (Amoss and Minoli, 2008). As with the other uses of dual-stack, the IPv4 and IPv6 protocols are not suitable with each other. The dual-stack design allows the simplest shifting from IPv4 to IPv6 environments with the minimal support interruptions. This design performs by allowing IPv6 in the current IPv4 environments along with the associated functions needed to create IPv6 routable, always available, and secured.

The main advantages of the dual-stack mechanism is, it doesn't need tunneling within the network topology. The dual-stack operates the two protocols as "ships-in-the-night," significance that IPv4 and IPv6 run together with one another and have no reliance on each other to operate, except that they share and use network properties. Both IPv4 and IPv6 have separate routing, High Availability (HA), Quality of Service (QoS), security, and multicast policies.

Dual-stack also provides sending efficiency advantages because packets are natively submitted without demanding extra encapsulation and search expense. The nodes in dual-stack assisting both protocols loads (IPv4 and IPv6), allowing them to be modeled with both IPv4 and IPv6 addresses (Blanchet, 2000). The dual-stack nodes use IPv4 and IPv6 networks such as Dynamic Host Configuration Protocol (DHCP) to obtain their specific requirements like addresses.

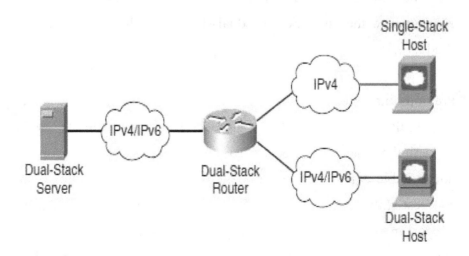

Figure 12: Dual-stack topology of IPv6

IPv6-over-IPv4 Tunnels

IPv4 is the prominent IP protocol implemented in the enterprise network fields. As the adaptation and implementation of IPv6 has been developed, IPv6 servers or whole features of the network might need to connect over IPv6 end to end, but IPv4-only fields the network in this way. This is difficult in WAN/branch deployments, where the branch and head-end servers are IPv6-enabled, but the WAN in between facilitates only IPv4 technology.

IPv6-over-IPv4 tunnels encapsulate IPv6 datagram within of IPv4, allowing end-to-end connection. Point-to-point or point-to-multipoint tunnels have been used to "carry" or tunnel one protocol, in this condition IPv6 over another protocol (IPv4) (Blanchet, 2000).

This tunnel network has been used for many decades to back up Novell IPX/SPX, AppleTalk, SNA, and others. There are 3 types of IPv6-over-IPv4 Tunnels they are discussed below:

- **Router-to-router:** In router-to-router tunneling, routers connected over IPv4 network can tunnel IPv6 packets by encapsulating these IPv6 packets inside the IPv4 header.

- **Host-to-router:** In host-to-router tunneling, the IPv4/IPv6 servers can tunnel the IPv6 packets to an IPv4/IPv6 border router.

This tunneling ends at the border router and from there on is sent natively over IPv6 to the end process.

- **Host-to-host:** In host-to-host tunneling, the tunnel prevails between the two or more hosts. The IPv6/IPv4 servers use the tunnel to connect among themselves by tunneling IPv6 packets within the IPv4 header (Blanchet, 2000).

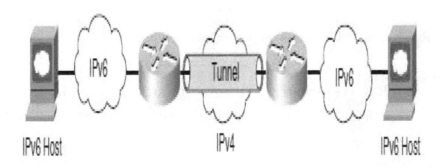

Figure 13: IPv6-over-IPv4 Tunneling topology

A table of IPv6-over-IPv4 Tunnels method is as follows:

Method	Description	Limitations (if any)
Manually configured tunnels	Supported by all implementations. Standards-based (RFC 4213).	Difficult to manage as the number of sites increases the operation effort increases exponentially as due to increase in number of sites the number of tunnels increases if fully mesh connections are desired (scalability).
IPv6-over-IPv4 GRE tunnel	Uses IPv4 GRE tunnels. From a tunnel configuration perspective, this is same as Manually Configured Tunnels.	Same as Manually Configured Tunnels.
Tunnel broker	Standards-based (RFC 3053). Requires dedicated tunnel brokers. Dynamic tunnels.	Tunnel broker service needs to accept configuration changes remotely, which leads to security implications.
6to4 tunnel	Standards-based (RFC 3056). Automatic tunneling. Uses IPv4 infrastructure such as a virtual broadcast link. Uses 2002::/16 as a prefix.	Underlying IPv4 address determines the 6to4 IPv6 address prefix, so migration to native IPv6 requires renumbering. Requires public IPv4 addressing. Doesn't support NAT along the path. No multicast support.
ISATAP	Automatic overlay mechanism (RFC 5214). Uses underlying IPv4 as non-broadcast multiaccess (NBMA) link. Easy to configure and can scale to large numbers of hosts.	Transport layer NAT not supported. Delimitation of IPv4 virtual link is required for security reasons. No multicast support.
IPv6 over MPLS	Uses existing MPLS infrastructure to transport IPv6.	Flexible but could be cumbersome to configure based on the underlying method used.

Figure 14: A table of IPv6-over-IPv4 Tunnels methods

IPv6 over MPLS

While the large enterprises gradually move their network to back up IPv6, they can use their current IPv4 MPLS system to tunnel IPv6. In this situation, the Provider Edge (PE) routers have the IPv6 routing ability, but the Provider (P) routers have no IPv6 routing services (connectivity between the separated IPv6 domains) without improving their central source networks.

The following table shows the various types of IPv6 over MPLS methods:

Method	Description	Limitations (if any)
IPv6 over circuit transport over MPLS	Service provider (SP) with circuit to CE (forexample, Frame Relay or ATM).	Scalability.
IPv6 using IPv4 tunnels over CE routers	This is a tunnel-in-tunnel approach and requires CE routers to be dual-stack enabled. No impact on the MPLS infrastructure. IPv6 traffic is encapsulated twice: first in the IPv4 packet and then into an MPLS frame.	Tunnel overhead.
IPv6 MPLS with IPv4-based core (6PE/6VPE)	Standards-based: RFC 4659, 6VPE RFC 4798, 6PE The service is provided over the existing IPv4 MPLS service. Only the PE routers are impacted.	Complexity. MPLS core doesn't know about IPv6. Hard to troubleshoot.

Figure 15: A table of IPv6 over MPLS methods

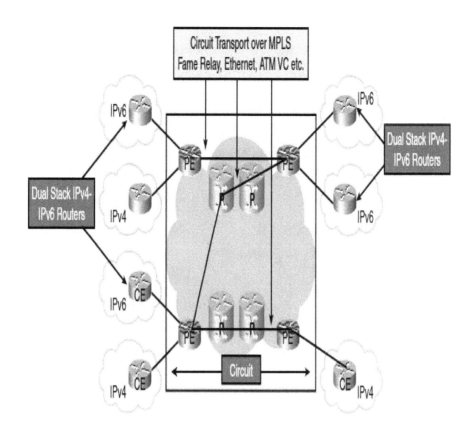

Figure 16: IPv6 over MPLS topology

3.2.3 Protocol Transition/Proxy Mechanisms

There are some analyzed situations that might need the power to translate or proxy between IPv4 and IPv6. For example, interpretation in the data center is necessary to allow connection between IPv6-enabled servers in the campus or branch and legacy IPv4-only servers in the data center accessibility section.

An advanced devices or node (for example, router, firewall application, or load balancer)) can translate from IPv4 to IPv6 and the other way around. Or the OS is capable of operating transition at the each endpoint (Leavitt, 2011). Some examples of networks that execute transition of IPv4/IPv6 includes:

- Network Address Transition: Protocol Transition (NAT-PT)
- NAT64
- TCP-UDP Relay
- Bump in the stack (BIS)
- SOCKS-based IPv6/IPv4 gateway

NAT-PT and NAT64 have been mentioned in this book because they are the most widely used mechanisms. Other mechanisms are not very popular, so they aren't discussed in this book

NAT-PT

NAT-PT works transition of the network layer addresses (Layer 3) between IPv4 and IPv6. In this procedure, end nodes in the IPv6 network are trying to connect with the nodes in the IPv4 network.

This strategy is mainly used for connection between the servers that are IPv6-only to the ones that are IPv4-only. NAT-PT uses a share of IPv4 addresses and designates them to IPv6 end nodes/hosts at the IPv4-IPv6 limitations. This procedure is just like present NAT mechanisms in IPv4 network (Leavitt, 2011).

NAT-PT is a Stateless IP/ICMP Transition (SIIT) algorithm, as defined in RFC 2765. This algorithm converts between the IPv4 and IPv6 packet headers without requiring any per connection condition.

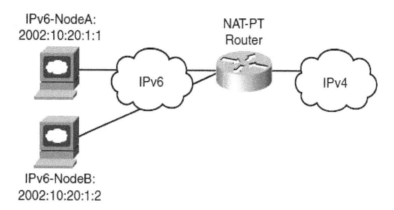

Before Translation		After Translation	
Source Address	Destination Address	Source Address	Destination Address
2002:10:20:1:1	2002:CAFO:1:1	192.168.1.1	10.12.1.1
2002:10:20:1:2	2002:CAFO:1:2	192.168.1.2	10.12.1.2

Figure 17: an example topology design for NAT-PT

NAT64:

As the name indicates, the NAT64 transition mechanism represents the interpretation of the IPv6 packet to an IPv4 packet. In the condition of NAT64, the initiator of the packet is always on the IPv6 section. Although NAT64 stores some of the same problems as the other NAT mechanisms.

It is the best choice because it is designed upon the years of confronting with IPv4 NAT. And NAT64 triumphs over some of the process of the other mechanisms like NAT-PT. NAT64 provides extra functions like NAT mapping, filtration, and TCP multiple start features, which are needed for the peer-to-peer environment. NAT64 also provides functions such as hairpinning, which allows the IPv6 servers and the NAT64 mechanisms to connect with each other.

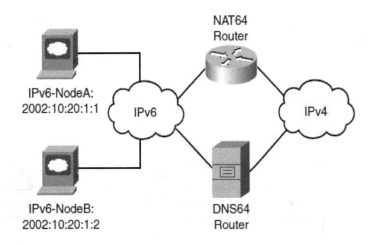

Figure 18: A network topology design for NAT64 transition mechanism

3.3 Enterprise IPv6 Network Services

Another implementation of enterprise IPv6 to utilize the network services. Enterprise networks nowadays require various network services in addition to data transmitting to bring staffs, clients, and stakeholders together.

It can increase worker efficiency while reducing overall costs of the enterprise. This can be achieved by allowing Multicast, Quality of Service (QoS) and IPv6 routing network services. The discussion of the network services are as follows:

3.3.1 Multicast

Multicast transmissions are a process, in this process source sends one duplicate copy of each packet to a special address that can be used by several receivers connected to that transmitting. Those sources and receivers are members of a specific multicast group and can be found anywhere on the network. Multicast-enabled network devices duplicate a copy of the packet to several receivers instead of each receiver having a devoted unicast communication with the source.

Using multicast to transmit graphical or video traffic decreases the overall network load and decreases the impact on the source of it, which is related to the needless duplication of a common data flow (Leavitt, 2011). Examples of applications that take advantage of multicast include video conferencing, enterprise emails, online or distance learning, and submission of software, stock index, and news. Modern receivers can be members of more than one group and must clearly be a part of a group before getting content. Because multicast traffic depends on User Datagram Protocol (UDP), which, compared with TCP, which has no built-in stability procedure such as:

Circulation control or error recovery mechanisms, sources such as QoS can enhance the stability of a multicast transmitting.

Some modern receivers can connect with the media server using unicast or multicast communications. The use of multicast has some advantages when a video stream is to be stored in several media servers. Because only a stream is needed from the IP based cameras or those types of encoders.

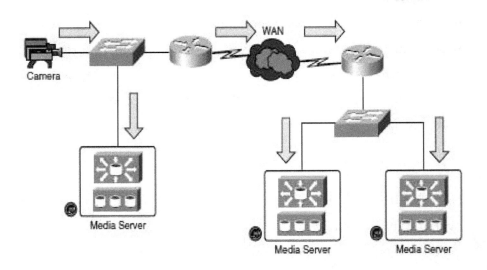

Figure 19: A diagram of Multicast based video surveillance transmission mechanism

3.3.2 Quality of Service (QoS)

At present, the enterprise networks are developed as per the complicated international communication model (Amoss and Minoli, 2008).

These networks are the platform to allow lots of applications, programs, services and solutions.

QoS protocols have the process of offering different program sources with the basic features and analytics such as Bandwidth, Delay, Interpacket wait difference (jitter), Packet loss. The following segment differentiates IPv6 and IPv4 QoS Mechanisms, IPv4 and IPv6 headers, IPv4 and IPv6 coexistence. This provides a better understanding of QoS operations for both protocols. This is useful when preparing for network shifting. The following table shows the difference between IPv6 and IPv4 QoS, Mechanisms:

QoS Mechanism	Implementation	IPv4	IPv6
Classification	Precedence	Y	Y
	DSCP	Y	Y
Marking	Class-based marking	Y	Y
	Committed Access Rate	Y	Y
	Policy-based routing	Y	Y
Policing and shaping	Rate limiting	Y	Y
	Class-based policing	Y	Y
	Generic traffic shaping	Y	N
	Frame Relay traffic shaping	Y	Y
Congestion avoidance	Weighted Random Early Detection	Y	Y
Congestion management	First In First Out	Y	Y
	Priority queuing	Y	Y (Legacy method not supported)
	Custom queuing	Y	N
	Low-latency queuing	Y	Y

Figure 20: Difference between IPv6 and IPv4 QoS, Mechanisms

The following table shows the difference between IPv4 and IPv6 headers:

IPv4 Header Field	IPv6 Header Field
Version	Different version number. Field is the same.
Header Length	Removed in IPv6. Fixed at 40 bytes.
Total Length	Payload Length.
Identification, Flags, Fragment Offset	Removed in IPv6.
Time-to-Live (TTL)	Hop Limit.
Protocol	Next Header.
Header Checksum	Removed in IPv6.
Source Address	Source Address (size is 128 bits).
Destination Address	Destination Address (size is 128 bits).
Options	Removed with IPv6 extension headers.
Type of Service	Traffic Class.

Figure 21: Difference between IPv4 and IPv6 headers

Difference between IPv4 and IPv6 Coexistence

There are two strategy in the coexistence of IPv4 and IPv6:

1. IPv6 traffics are handled in a different way than IPv4 by using two different QoS guidelines.

2. IPv6 traffics are handled the same as IPv4 by using only one QoS strategy that categorizes and supports on both protocols.

The Per Hop Behaviors (PHB) for the two protocols might be different under the following way:

1. IPv4 traffics are generating profit and it is more essential for the enterprise than the IPv6 traffics, at least in the beginning. In that situation, an enterprise might select the IPv6 traffics reducing strategy and offer less sources for it (Amoss and Minoli, 2008).

2. IPv4 and IPv6 traffic might have to notice different PHBs based on traffics designs used by the various applications.

In these situations, different policies and guidelines should be mentioned for each traffic type. In transition mechanisms, IPv6 traffics can make use of the used QoS of the deployed IPv4 system. In some conditions, the IPv6 traffics might also reduce its percentage after traversing the IPv4 protocol.

3.3.3 IPv6 Routing

Several IPv4 Routing Protocol (RP) is available for discovering channels between network, and almost every one of them has an IPv6 bookmark or extension. The following routing protocols are used for IPv6 routing:

- Open Shortest Path First version 3 (OSPFv3)

- Routing Information Protocol next-generation (RIPng)
- Intermediate Network–to–Intermediate Network (ISIS)
- Enhanced Architecture
- Gateway Routing Protocol (EIGRP)
- EIGRPv6
- Border Gateway Protocol (BGP)

As the in-depth discussion of the routing protocols are very vast, so the author has only discussed about the OSPFv3, IS-IS, EIGRPv6, and Border Gateway Protocol (BGP) routing protocols. These routing protocols are widely used in the enterprise IPv6 network development. The discussions are as follows:

OSPFv3

The Open Shortest Path First (OSPF) is a type of connection state protocol. OSPFv2 is an Interior Gateway Protocol (IGP) used to send routing information between routers of a single independent network of IPv4 network.

The updates for IPv6 were found in OSPF version 3 (OSPFv3). Routers operating OSPF promotes connection state, connect prefix/mask, connect weight and other native connectivity factors in Link State Advertisement (LSA).

These LSAs is filled effectively to other routers in the network to make sure that every OSPF router has a finish and reliable perspective of the topology (Amoss and Minoli, 2008).

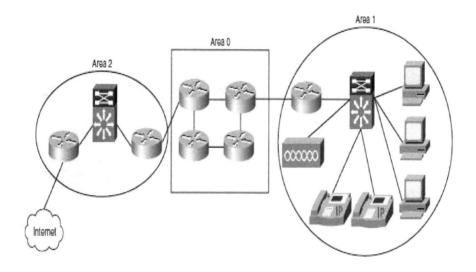

Figure 22: The communication process of Open Shortest Path First (OSPF) IPv6 routing protocol

IS-IS

The Intermediate Network–to–Intermediate Network (IS-IS) protocol is described in ISO Standard 10589. This connects-state, OSI routing was not initially designed for IP but rather to offer the routing performance between the routers of Connectionless Network Protocol (CLNP) based networks.

With the inclusion of IPv4 assistance (RFC 1195), the protocol sometimes generally known as Incorporated IS-IS (I/IS-IS), was commonly use as the IGP for many ISP and large enterprise networks (Blanchet, 2000).

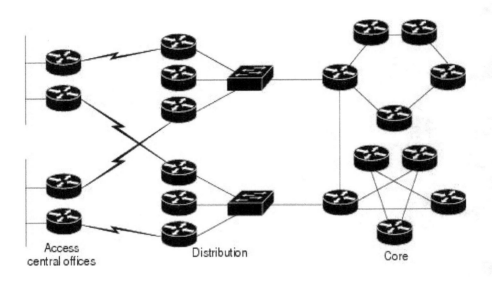

Figure 23: The communication process of Intermediate Network –to–Intermediate Network (IS-IS) IPv6 routing protocol

EIGRPv6

The EIGRPv6 is a distance vector routing protocol depending on IGRP. This edition comes from Cisco-proprietary Enhanced Interior Gateway Protocol (EIGRP) that was designed to connect the gap between the traditional distance vector protocols (IGRP, RIP) and the advance connect state protocols (OSPF, IS-IS).

It combines some of the confirmed abilities of the latter to enhance the function and the scalability of the past distance vector routing protocol (Blanchet, 2000).

The purpose was to prevent some of the topological restrictions that are sometimes associated with connect-state protocols. The outcome is fast-converging, long lasting, and scalable routing protocol that is mostly implemented in many enterprise networks and some ISP networks as well.

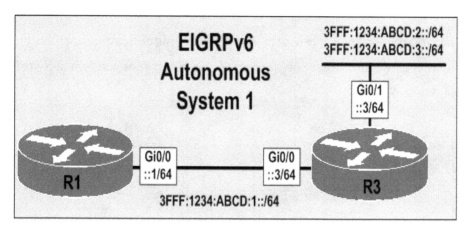

Figure 24: EIGRPv6 routing protocol independent network communication process

BGP

Border Gateway Protocol edition 4 (BGP4) is the External Gateway Protocol (EGP) used to return channels between independent technology in the Internet. BGP was developed depending on interaction obtained with EGP, and provides built-in assistance for CIDR and route aggregation. BGP4 is specified in RFC 1771 and other BGP related documents: RFC 1772, RFC 1773, and RFC 1774.

BGP can be implemented in two forms: i. exterior BGP (eBGP) and ii. interior BGP (iBGP). eBGP is used for inter–independent network peering, whereas iBGP provides BGP direction addresses within the same independent network (Leavitt, 2011).

Although some of the addresses (route, metric) taken by iBGP might be repetitive with that promoted by IGPs such as IS-IS, OSPF, and so on. It's true that, no IGP is able to replace BGP specific path attributes such as the 'AS_PATH'. Hence, iBGP is necessary to make sure that the BGP path attributes obtained on an advantage of the independent network over the eBGP communications, which are available on the other advantage of the same independent network (Leavitt, 2011).

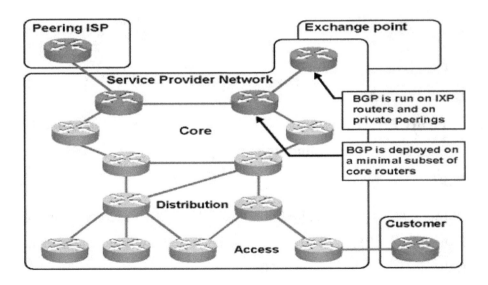

Figure 25: BGP routing protocol independent network communication process

Testing

3.4 Enterprise IPv6 Network Deployment in Practical Scenario

In this segment, the author has shown an enterprise IPv6 network deployment process in a practical scenario. For that reason the author has shown an example enterprise, which needs to deploy enterprise IPv6 based network in their small enterprise. Suppose the name of this small enterprise is "ABC Enterprise". The ABC Enterprise wants to upgrade their network system for various types of enterprise related purposes. So the enterprise has been chosen Enterprise IPv6 Network solution.

There are several types of enterprise IPv6 network deployment methods are presently available:

- Deploying IPv6 in Campus Networks
- Deploying Virtualized IPv6 Networks
- Deploying IPv6 in WAN/Branch Networks
- Deploying IPv6 in the Data Center
- Deploying IPv6 for Remote Access VPN

From the above enterprise IPv6 network deployment methods, ABC Enterprise has been chosen IPv6 in Campus Networks deployment methods. Because Campus Networks deployment method is effective for any Campus Network Design based enterprise network. As ABC Enterprise follows the Enterprise IPv6 Campus Network Design structure for their network development, hence they chose this deployment method.

It is an effective network deployment method for small enterprise. It is a cheaper method than the other methods. And the network management, address management, Multicast, scalability, performance, etc. features is quite invincible than the other deployment methods. This method has been developed based on Enterprise Campus Network Design.

3.4.1 Enterprise IPv6 Campus Network Deployment Models

There are several Enterprise IPv6 Campus Network Deployment Models are available in Campus Network deployment. Their names and features are as follows:

- **Dual-stack Model (DSM):** In this model, both IPv4 and IPv6 are implemented at the same time on the same connections.

- **Hybrid Model (HM):** The Host-based tunneling model is used to encapsulate IPv6 in IPv4 when required, and dual-stack is used everywhere else.

- **Service Block Model (SBM):** SBM is just like the hybrid design, only tunnel termination happens in a purpose-built aspect of the network known as the service block.

From those above models, ABC Enterprise has selected Dual-stack Model (DSM), because of its IPv4 and IPv6 dual-stack transition mechanisms. The discussion of Dual-stack mechanism has already been done in the "3.2 Enterprise IPv6 Coexistence Mechanisms", so the author doesn't discuss it in this part of the book. But the author has discussed the advantages and limitations of Dual-stack Model (DSM) in the following segment.

3.4.2 Reason behind Choosing Dual-stack Model (DSM)

ABC Enterprise has chosen Dual-stack Model (DSM) for its following advantages:

Advantages of Dual-stack Model (DSM)

Implementing IPv6 in the Campus Network design using DSM provides several advantages over the hybrid and service block models. The main advantages of DSM are that, it does not need tunneling within the campus network. DSM operates the two methods as "ships in the night," significance that IPv4 and IPv6 run together with one another and have no reliance on each other to operate, except that they share network resource. Both IPv4 and IPv6 have independent routing, security, multicast guidelines, High Availability (HA), Quality of Service (QoS), and security.

DSM also provides controlling efficiency advantages, because packets are natively submitted without having to the consideration for extra encapsulation and search overhead.

The following tables discuss the difference between Dual-Stack Model (DSM), Hybrid Model (HM), and Service Block Model (SBM)

Model	Benefit	Challenge
Dual-stack model (DSM)	No tunneling required No dependency on IPv4 Superior performance and highest availability for IPv6 unicast and multicast Scalable	Requires IPv6 hardware-enabled campus switching equipment Operational challenges with supporting dual protocols - training/management tools
Hybrid model (HM)	Most of the existing IPv4-only campus equipment can be used (access and distribution layer) Per-user or per-application control for IPv6-service delivery Provides high availability for IPv6 access over ISATAP tunnels	Tunneling is required; increase in operations and management Scale factors (number of tunnels, hosts per tunnel) IPv6 multicast is not supported Tunnel termination at core
Service block model (SBM)	Highly reduced time to delivery for IPv6-enabled services Requires no changes to existing campus infrastructure Similar to the HM in other advantages	New IPv6 hardware capable, campus switches are required All cons from the HM

Figure 26: Difference between Dual-Stack Model (DSM), Hybrid Model (HM), and Service Block Model (SBM)

Limitations of Dual-stack Model (DSM)

There are very few limitations of Dual-stack Model (DSM). ABC Enterprise had kept it in their mind at the time of selected this model. The limitations are as follows:

DSM limitation is less than the other models. The main disadvantage of DSM is that, network device improvements might be needed when the current networking devices are not IPv6 enabled. Also, there is an operational cost in working with two methods at the same time, because there are two places of everything, such as address, routing protocols, access control lists (ACL) etc.

3.4.3 Topology Design of ABC Enterprise

As ABC Enterprise has chosen Enterprise Campus Network Design and Dual-stack Model (DSM) for their network development, so they follow the DSM based Enterprise Campus Network topology.

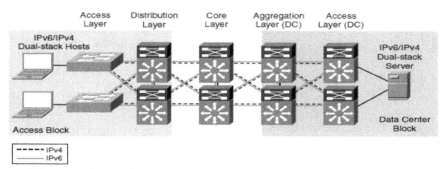

Figure 27: ABC Enterprise Dual-Stack Model Enterprise Campus Network topology

Figure 27, Shows, ABC Enterprise high-level objective of the DSM-based deployment in the Enterprise Campus Network. This topology has 5 layers, namely Distribution Layer, Access Layer, Core Layer, Aggregation Layer (DC) and Access Layer (DC). The environment is using a conventional tree-tier design, with an access, distribution, and core layer at the campus. All appropriate connections that have IPv4 enabled also have IPv6 enabled, making it a real dual-stack system and model as well.

3.4.4 Software and Components Test of ABC Enterprise DSM Campus Network Design

The author has shown some components and software test of ABC Enterprise DSM Campus Network Design. The following table shows the DSM Tested Components of ABC Enterprise Campus Network Design which are used for the development of the network:

Campus Layer	Hardware	Software
Access layer	Cisco Catalyst 3750E/3560E Catalyst 4500 Supervisor 6-E Catalyst 6500 Supervisor 32 or 720	12.2(46)SE 12.2(46)SG 12.2(33)SXI
Host devices	Various laptops: PC and Apple	Microsoft Windows XP, Windows Vista, Windows 7, Apple Mac OS X, and Red Hat Enterprise Linux WS
Distribution layer	Catalyst 4500 Supervisor 6-E Catalyst 6500 Supervisor 32 or 720	12.2(46)SG 12.2(33)SXI
Core layer	Catalyst 6500 Supervisor 720	12.2(33)SXI

Figure 28: DSM Tested Components of ABC Enterprise Campus Network

Dynamic Host Configuration Protocol (DHCP)

Dynamic Host Configuration Protocol (DHCP) software interface can identify the network configuration parameters. And can identify the Enterprise IPv6 deployed network models IP addresses for interfaces and services. IPv4 needs manual DHCP address configuration. But IPv6 can automatically do the DHCP address configuration tasks. The following figure shows ABC Enterprise DSM Campus Network automatic DHCP address configuration test result:

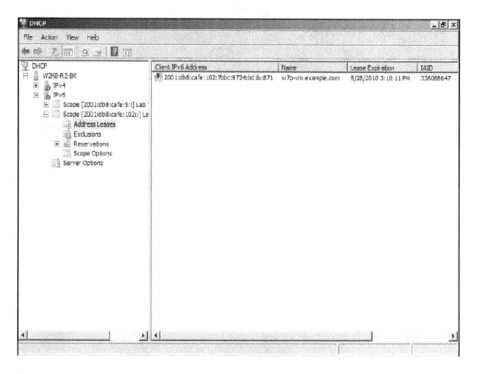

Figure 29: DHCP software interface shows ABC Enterprise IPv6 has been successfully passed the automatic Address Configuration Test

The author also has tested the ABC Enterprise DSM Campus Network File Transfer Protocol (FTP) environment by completing a simple CMD (Command Shell) analysis. The following figure shows the ABC Enterprise DSM Campus Network FTP over Enterprise IPv6 CMD (Command Shell) test result:

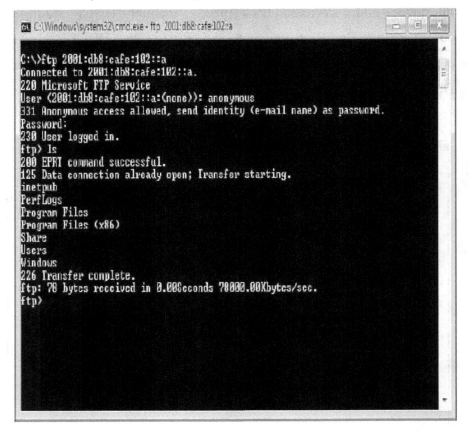

Figure 30: DSM Campus Network FTP over Enterprise IPv6 test

This test and implementation of the network demonstrate that ABC enterprise has been successfully implemented the IPv6 Campus Networks deployment methods as their enterprise networking solution.

3.4.5 Campus IPv6 Deployment Considerations

ABC Enterprise must consider the following conditions to deploy their DSM based Campus IPv6 Network Design:

Physical Connectivity: For the physical connectivity, it is necessary to consider sufficient bandwidth, connection of IPv6 with Maximum Transmission Unit (MTU) and Operating IPv6 over the WLAN. Along with these, the Enterprise has to consider the traffic profile, proper utilization of CPU and memory for both host and network.

VLANs: VLAN is similar for both IPv4 and IPv6 protocols. The ABC Enterprise should consider both the protocols similar for VLAN.

High Availability: ABC Enterprise should consider the three important functions, redundant routing and forwarding paths, availability of first-hop gateways and three layers of a switch.

QoS: QoS policy act as a keyword removing policy for both the protocols. IPv6 has a modern set of mechanism, so most of the keywords of IPv6 are different from the IPv4. So, this policy is necessary to ensure the best performance of the IPv6 keywords.

Addressing: The Enterprise developed an addressing table which is given below:

64 Bits	Greater Than 64 Bits	Less Than 64 Bits
Recommended by RFC 5375 and IAB/IESG	Address space conservation	Enables more hosts per broadcast domain
Consistency makes management easy	Special cases: - /126 - Valid for p2p - /127 - Valid for p2p if aware of overlapping addresses (RFC 3627) - /128 - Loopback	Considered bad practice
/64 required for SLAAC, SEND, and Privacy extensions	Complicates management	64 bits offers more space for hosts than media can support efficiently
Significant address space loss	Must avoid overlap with specific addresses: - Router Anycast (RFC 3513) - Embedded RP (RFC 3956)	No real justifiable use case for this option

Figure 31: 64 bit Addressing Table of DSM based Campus Network Design of ABC Enterprise

Routing: Enterprise IPv4 and IPv6 depend on Interior Gateway Protocol (IGP). Most of the functions of IGP are almost same for the both protocols. In some cases Enterprise IPv6 is used different functions of IGP. For better performance. For converging network, it is necessary to tune the IGP.

Multicast Configuration: ABC Enterprise has used DSM model, because it fully supports Multicast configuration.

To enable multicast on Enterprise IPv6 network an enterprise must consider Command Line Interface (CLI) input for general network setting. And for global setting it should enable PIM Source-Specific Multicast (PIM-SSM).

Security: ABC Enterprise should maintain high level security in their DSM Campus network deployment. As many common viruses, threats, worms, unauthorized access, malware, etc. attack the IPv4 networking models, hence these can also try to attack the IPv6. There are some Cisco security tools available in the market, ABC Enterprise can use those tools to secure their enterprise IPv6 DSM Campus network.

3.5 Answering the General Question

In this segment the author has been discussed about the following general question. That was shown in the research proposal:

What are the challenges in rolling out IPv6 across an enterprise network?

There are many challenges faced during rolling out IPv6 across an enterprise network. The challenges are given below:

Government Policy: Most of the governments of the developed nations prefer IPv4 networking solutions. As the IPv6 network solution is newly introduced, so those governments now prefer some features of IPv6 in their nations. Still, they like to consider the address of IPv4 in IPv6 protocol mechanism.

Preference for Mobile Devices: At present, most of the mobile companies prefer IPv4 for their devices, just fewer of them use the IPv6 technology. It is a great challenge for rolling out IPv6 over enterprise networks.

Higher Cost for Deployment: It remains costly to deploy IPv6 network design in a small enterprise because of its high price and operating cost.

Lack of Technological Knowledge on IPv6: Due to lack of proper knowledge about IPv6 network, many enterprises still use IPv4 for their enterprise purposes.

Inefficient Address Use: For the small enterprise, there is no need for high address capable network like IPv6. Using IPv6 will be regarded as an inefficient. So for those cases, IPv6 are usually ignored.

Excess Server Uses: As IPv6 has enhanced address options, hence it needs more storage. As a result, the enterprise needs to provide more servers for this technology, which is inefficient for small enterprises.

Lack of Skilled Workforce: Most of the enterprises have lack of skilled technical workforce. This creates challenges in rolling out IPv6 across an enterprise network.

Need of High Security: IPv6 is the upgraded version of IPv4, it needs more security tools than IPv4. This creates challenges in rolling out IPv6 across an enterprise network.

SIMULATIONS

4.0 Comparison between IPv6 and IPv4 Using Opnet Simulator

In this section the two internet protocols IPv6 and IPv4 have been compared by using OPNET as a simulation tool. OPNET stands for "Optimized Network Engineering Tool." It has the ability to simulate large communication networks. OPNET simulation software isn't a freeware, hence you have to purchase this software before doing any simulation.

The massive expansion of the internet in recent days has created most significant challenges in the addressing of the new hosts such as cell phone, laptop, tablets and smart phone.

These requirements have necessitated for the design of Internet Protocol Version 6 abbreviated as IPv6 (Hinden and Deering, 1998).

4.1 Simulation Process

In this section the IPv4 and IPv6 properties are evaluated in a very simple networking, which operates in a non-complex configuration. The IPv6 and IPv4 are implemented first in a basic network and then they are simulated on the campus network.

4.2 Simulation of IPv4 and IPv6 Networks with Voice Application

Setting up Differentiated Services in OpNet

By setting up differentiated Services in OpNet simulation software, the author can identify the Quality of Service (QoS) of IPv4 and IPv6.

As IPv4 is the old version of IP and the performance of the protocol is more limited than IPv6, so the author has shown the IPv4 as "Without QoS" in this simulation process.

In contrary, the author has selected IPv6 as "With QoS" because of its outstanding performance.

IPv4 Without QoS

At first, Opnet simulation software was selected for this simulation process. Then the author selected the Application configuration and Profile configuration from the Object Palette.

The author selected 2 main nodes which are connected to the end user. The organizing process of Application configuration and Profile configuration from the Object Palette are shown below:

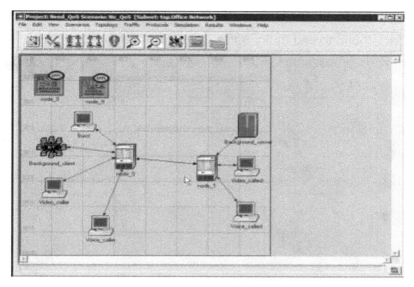

Figure 33: Selecting Application configuration and Profile configuration from the Object Palette

With the first node, three Ethernet Workstation was selected. One of them Burst Traffic, others are, Voice Caller and Video Caller. The author will mainly use the voice caller. 10 Base T Switched LAN was selected to be used as a background client. Node 2, have Video called, Voice called and the Background client as end user.

In App Config, the following steps are followed:
1.   Edit Attributes
2.   Application Definition
3.   Select Row 3
4.   Go to Description
5.   Voice PCM Quality Speech

To view the result the author selects the view result option and check the Packet end to end delay option.

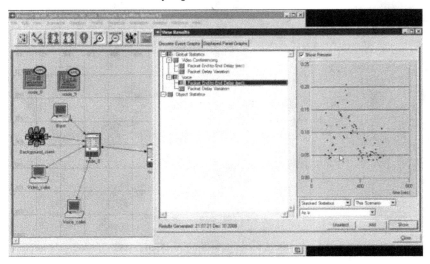

Figure 34: The simulation is showing quite high picks in Packet End to End Delay (sec) in IPv4 voice application packet transmission

The result is shown in a graphical manner. This is a simulation process done for without IPv4 QoS.

IPv6 With QoS:

For this task the author selected scenario option, then chose duplicate scenario to simulate the required result with QoS service. As, the author is using only voice conversation, he enabled the QoS only in between the voice caller and voice called end user. Then, the author selected the following steps:

1.   Protocols

2.   IP

3.   QoS

4.   Configure QoS

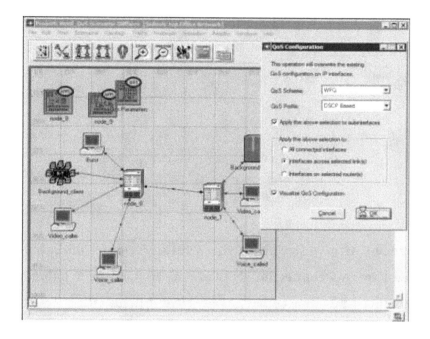

Figure 35: Selecting WFQ (Weighted For Queue) queue system as QoS Scheme and DSCP (Differentiated Service Code Point) Based as QoS Profile

In the configuration, WFQ (Weighted For Queue) queue system was selected as QoS Scheme and DSCP (Differentiated Service Code Point) Based was selected as QoS Profile. A new IP node appears which is named as QoS Parameter. In the edit attribute option of QoS parameter, all types of configuration can be checked.

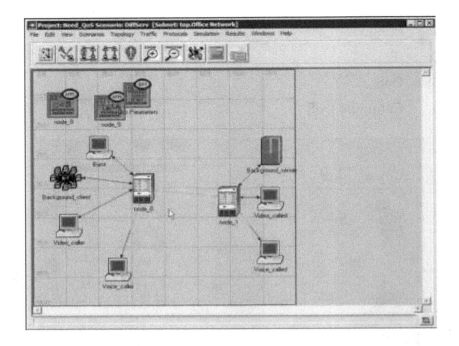

Figure 36: After selecting all type configurations from attribute, the end to end connection between node 0, node 1 along with voice caller and voice called have turned into green

Now before the final simulation, the author followed the following steps,

1. App configuration
2. Edit Attributes
3. App Definition
4. Row3
5. Description
6. Voice
7. Value (Edit)

8.   Type of Service (Interactive Voice)

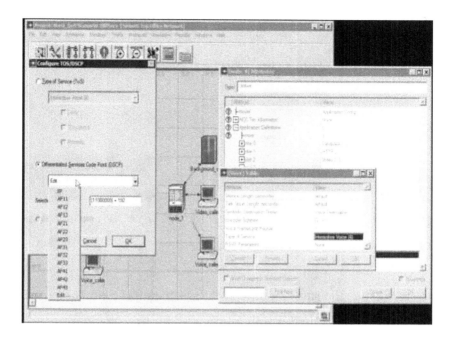

Figure 37: Configuring TOS/DSCP, DSCP is marked as check

and EF is selected

A window pops having a name Configure TOS/DSCP. DSCP was marked as check. And EF was selected. Now to simulate the author selects Configuration Simulation need_ QoS and selects run option from it. And the simulation with QoS starts.

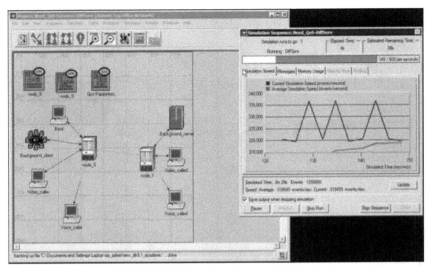

Figure 38: Showing the simulation of IPv6 in voice packet transmission with QoS

After it finishes the same option was chosen as discussed above to view results. This time the authors found that the graphical representation shows a straight line for IPv6 with QoS.

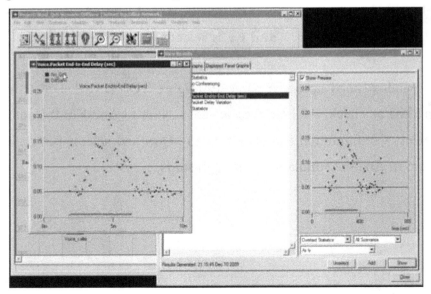

Figure 39: The simulation is shown that, the blue scattered dots are the voice packet End to End Delay (sec) of IPv4 these are shown here as "No_QoS" where, the red straight line dots are the voice packet End to End Delay (sec) of IPv6 those are shown as "Diffserv".

Whereas, in the graphical representation of IPv4 (without) QoS the graph was scattered. For comparing the both scenarios all the scenarios options was marked as check.

For above comparison, the author has tried to prove that, IPv6 End to End Delay (sec) in voice packet transmission is very much stable and faster than IPv4 voice packet transmission.

Thus the comparison between IPv4 (without QoS) and IPv6 (with QoS) is simulated. And from the result, it can be very easily identified that IPv6 have a clear advantages over IPv4 in not only voice application packet transmission but also all the other packet transmission.

5.0 Critical Evaluation

The author has found following critical evaluations from the overall research and he has presented these evaluations in this book:

- ❖ IPv6 is usually very costly and occupies large space, hence it is really inefficient for small size enterprise.

- ❖ On the other hand, some large scale enterprises are already using enterprise IPv6 for their growing enterprise purposes.

- ❖ IPv6 offers large address space for the user, so the govt. of developed nations have already made some policies to implement this technology in their territories.

- ❖ Most OS and Apps are now supporting IPv6 protocols by default, so it is now very demandable in technology areas.

- ❖ Most of the enterprise software is now supporting IPv6 protocol and addresses. The world famous technology companies like Google, Apple, Microsoft, Oracle, Amazon, etc. have already implemented this technology.

- ❖ In recent years, it is observed that the developing nation's enterprises are trying to implement IPv6 in their enterprise network. So it is very clear that in the near future IPv6 will rule the entire networking systems of the world.

6.0 Conclusion

The transition to IPv6 will take much shorter time from now and till then IPv4 and IPv6 should co-exist. Some firms may not prepare for leaving IPv4 and adopting IPv6 fully within short time. So inter connecting networks and devices across heterogeneous environments will be a major recommendation. Because IPv6 is an industry standard networking technology. So the necessary hardware and software applications produced by different vendors in the market should in accordance with that standard should be interoperable. That means the protocol will not stop the devices in interpreting.

There may be some interoperability problems, but that will be limited. Because manufacturer of the networking components and devices will quickly adjust to avoid any productivity issues and associated damages from interoperability problems that may arise when use IPv4 and IPv6 devices together. Many researchers have shown that no obvious problems arise in implementing the IETF standards for IPv6 because major operating system and router vendors already have implemented and periodically demonstrated interoperability.

For that reason, government should involve in co-coordinating and supporting the development of standards, protocols and conformance of IPv6. Government should be an active participant in identifying and facilitating technical solutions and interoperability solutions. Government should act as a best consumer to the IPv6 products and technologies and should become an example maker for others.

Industry also should take active participation, develop standards and technologies along with help the government in this process. From the above research work we found out the following facts about IPv6.

(1) It is a complex standard. It consists of a suite of protocols, lots of new definitions, new transition mechanisms, and lot of operational procedures. The advantages of IPv6 over IPv4 will vary depends on so many factors.

(2) A collection of strategies like NATing was introduced in IPv4 to resolve the less IP addresses problems in IPv4. This won't work in most of the applications like smart phones.

(3) IPv6 stakeholders will be developed Infrastructure (Hardware and Software) Vendors, Application Vendors, Internet Service Providers (ISPs) and Internet Users. The entire factor associated with IPv6 upgradation will vary depends on from which group the stakeholder is ready to implement it.

(4) There should be a good public-private co-ordination in the development of IPv6. Government should act as an example maker and should act as a pioneer and a major customer of IPv6 products.

In this book at the first part a detail discussion was done about the objective and goal of this research. Besides, the background of this book was also given some light. The reason why this topic selected and the importance of this topic in practical works are all well explained in the first part.

The second part on the other hand discussed about the artifact and the way the total work done on the book. The second part started with a detailed discussion on the artifact and its execution procedures. IPv6 follows some definite network designs. There are few different network designs with its unique features. These network designs have discussed properly along with the figures. After the designs, the mechanisms for the protocols to co-exist side by side were explained. Dual stack was recommended as the transition mechanism for IPv4 and IPv6. Network transitions and services as well as its considerations were also recommended for a safe approach in using IPv6.

Next, the important step was the deployment of the IPv6 network system. The book worked as a definite network designing guide to show its practical use in an enterprise network environment. As a result, only one design was chosen for the book. The design chosen was Campus Network design. And the DSM model was chosen for the deployment purpose.

The reason Campus Network was chosen because it is more feasible for small enterprises and its deployment mechanisms are less costly and easy to do all the setup. Using IPv6 and maintaining is a difficult task. The enterprise should consider some important and key points for smoothly running the protocol IPv6. These points were discussed in details in this book. Finally, the general question was answered in the last segment, which is related to the topic. In the general questions segment the answer covered some problem faced during rolling out the IPv6 protocol.

In the general questions segment, the answer covered some problem faced during rolling out the IPv6 protocol. Besides, the difference between IPv4 and IPv6 were presented in ways to show how IPv6 differs from the previous version. This concludes the analysis. Some researchers till feel that the existing IPv4 can be upgraded at a less cost instead of going for IPv6. This is somehow like a chicken and egg scenario. IPv6 is better than updating existing IPv4. The government should work to build the necessary base of skilled human resources for the development of IPv6. Government can ensure the IPv6-enabled services are deployed in a timely manner.

The Government can fund for the advanced testbed deployment of IPv6, should be made available and advertised appropriately for the better growth and utilization of IPv6 in the enterprise network development.

References

Amoss, J. and Minoli, D. (2008). *Handbook of IPv4 to IPv6 transition*. Boca Raton: Auerbach Publications.

Bouras, C., Karaliotas, A. and Ganos, P. (2003). The deployment of IPv6 in an IPv4 world and transition strategies. *Internet Research*, 13(2), pp.86-93.

Blanchet, M. (2000). *IP addressing and subnetting, including IPv6*. Rockland, MA: Syngress Media.

Draves, R. (2003), "Default Address Selection for Internet Protocolversion 6 (IPv6)", RFC 3484.

Hossain, G.M. (2013). *IPv4 IPv6 Technology and Implementation*. Dhaka: Amazon Create Space. 10-40.

Hinden, R. and S. Deering (2003), "Internet ProtocolVersion 6 (IPv6) Addressing Architecture", RFC 3513.

Kim, J. (2011). IPv6 Migration, OSPFv3 Routing based on IPv6, and IPv4/IPv6 Dual-Stack Networks and IPv6 Network: Modeling, and Simulation. *The KIPS Transactions: PartC*, 18C (5), pp.343-360.

Lawson, S. (2011). *Update: ICANN assigns its last IPv4 Addresses.* New York: Computerworld. 20-50.

Leavitt, N. (2011). IPv6: Any Closer to Adoption? *Computer*, 44(9), pp.14-16.

M. Bagnulo and F. Baker. (2008). IPv4/IPv6 Co-existence and Transition. *Requirements for Solutions.* 71 (3), 12-33.

McFarland, S. (2011). *IPv6 for enterprise networks.* Indianapolis: Cisco Press.

Sholomon, A. and Kunath, T. (2011). *Enterprise network testing.* Indianapolis, IN: Cisco Press.

T. Rooney (2011). *Service Provider IPv6 Deployment Strategies.* Lisbon: BT Diamond IP. 36-92.

The Cisco Network. (2014). *The ABCs of IP version 6 Technical Book.* [internet] available from <http://www.cisco.com/warp/public/732/abc/docs/abcIPv6> [21th MAR 2014]

About the Author

Ghazi Mokammel Hossain is a professional e-book, article, research, analysis paper and a creative writer. He has written some books as well as many articles, research papers, analysis and creative articles. The author is also a freelance writer as well as a researcher. The author lives in Dhaka, Bangladesh. He was born on 31 December 1993. The name of his father is Ghazi Mozammel Hossain and his mother's name is Syeda Taskin Ara. He has passed his S.S.C exam from Dhaka under Dhaka Board in 2008 and passed his H.S.C exam from Dhaka under Dhaka Board in 2010. He has graduated with a Bachelor's of Business Administration in HRM in 2015 from a renowned University. He has also completed Computer Science and Engineering certificate course in 2011.

He published his first book called "IPv4 IP6 Technology & Implementation" in Amazon Kindle and Createspace on 2013. The author published his second book called "Introduction to Network on Chip Routing Algorithms" in 2014. He also published "Fundamental of API Based Financial Engineering" and "Ebola Epidemic: A Detail Survival Guide From Ebola Virus Disease Outbreak" in 2014. The author published an outstanding thrilling novel called "The Survival of USA" in 2015 on Amazon kindle and Createspace. Playing football, Cricket, PC games, reading books, novel, research paper, cycling and mountain climbing are his favorite hobbies. For more details please visit Amazon Author Central: amazon.com/author/ghazimokammelhossain

www.ingramcontent.com/pod-product-compliance
Lightning Source LLC
Chambersburg PA
CBHW061014050326
40689CB00012B/2638